DISCARD

√98

Our Vanishing
FARM ANIMALS

Saving America's Rare Breeds

BY CATHERINE PALADINO

Little, Brown and Company
Boston   Toronto   London

For all those who tend the earth's rare creatures

The author gratefully acknowledges:
Carolyn Christman and the staff of the American Minor Breeds Conservancy, whose thoughtful,
enthusiastic correspondence and tireless efforts on behalf of rare livestock breeds helped make this book possible;
the many livestock breed associations that generously shared their valuable resources;
and the farmers and families who took time out of their busy lives to be a part of this book, without whom,
of course, it wouldn't exist.

Special thanks to the following institutions for providing animals for photographs:
Boston MDC MetroParks Zoos (Franklin Park Zoo) for their Ancona hens and White Jersey Giant rooster;
Codman Community Farms of Lincoln, Massachusetts, for their Devon calf; and Plimoth Plantation of
Plymouth, Massachusetts, for its Dorking hens and San Clemente goats.

Library of Congress Cataloging-in-Publication Data

Paladino, Catherine.
Our vanishing farm animals: saving America's rare breeds / by Catherine Paladino. — 1st ed.
  p.   cm.
Summary: Focuses on eight rare breeds of endangered farm animals, imported from all parts of the world and raised on
small family farms.
ISBN 0-316-68891-6
1. Domestic animals — United States — Genetics — Juvenile literature.   2. Animal breeding — United States — Juvenile
literature.   3. Rare animals — United States — Juvenile literature.   [1. Domestic animals.   2. Animal breeding.   3. Rare
animals.]   I. Title.
SF105.P28   1991
636'.00973 — dc20   90-42828

Joy Street Books are published by Little, Brown and Company (Inc.)
10 9 8 7 6 5 4 3 2 1
SC

Published simultaneously in Canada
by Little, Brown & Company (Canada) Limited

Printed in Hong Kong

Introduction

Never have we been more aware of the plight of endangered animals than we are today. But when we think of rare animals, elephants, leopards, or other wild beasts usually come to mind; cows, horses, and pigs seem too ordinary to be in danger of going extinct. Yet over half of our breeds of farm animals exist in such small numbers that soon they could be gone forever.

How did this happen? Like any business, agriculture follows trends. Farm animals fall in and out of fashion, and more modern breeds replace older ones. Today's commercial farms focus on those animals that produce the most, whether their product is milk, wool, or eggs. Modern breeds generally excel in only one function: beef cattle produce beef, and milking cattle produce milk. These are called single-purpose animals. But old-fashioned breeds were often multipurpose animals. For instance, Red Devon cattle, most famous for their Devonshire cream, provided milk, meat, and the muscle-power to pull the farmer's plow.

While the older breeds may not produce as much as their modern counterparts, they tend to require less feed, less shelter, and less veterinary care. Many of these breeds first came to America with settlers and traders from other countries. Because of the harsh conditions of early farm life, old-fashioned animals were bred to survive droughts, floods, and blizzards with little or no shelter. Having grown accustomed over the years to barren, rocky pastures, these breeds thrive on low-quality forage. Many of them have developed a resistance to things that would make modern breeds sick, such as foot rot and internal parasites. In a world where the amount of available grassland is shrinking, the population is growing, and economic conditions are changing, these traits may very well become valuable again.

In fact, our older breeds are a vital resource simply because they provide a *variety* of genetic traits. Agriculture today relies mostly on a few major livestock breeds. If a flu epidemic struck any of these breeds, a major source of our everyday food could be wiped out. The hardier breeds could provide a solution to this problem; with them, a farmer could rebuild a devastated herd or flock, or even build a new, less vulnerable one. Unless we take care to preserve our old-fashioned breeds, however, they will vanish, along with their unique genetic traits, which may hold answers to the future of farming in America.

The natural intelligence, friendliness, and adaptability of old-fashioned breeds make them ideal homestead animals. Indeed, small family farms may be their best hope for survival. This book tells the stories of a handful of rare-breed farmers and their families; without children and adults like them, more of the world's endangered animals could be lost.

Dutch Belted Cow

D own the hill, near a scattering of red and white barns in a green field, the cows graze. A small sign tells what kind they are: Dutch Belted dairy cows. This is Diamond Heart Farm in Vermont. Seventy-five Dutch Belts live here; they are cared for by Farmer Paul Daniels and his wife, Nancy.

Most of the Dutch Belts are black and white, but several are reddish-brown and white. They're not ordinary-looking, however. Compared to the usual spotted Holstein cows you pass on the way here, Dutch Belts look strikingly different. Dark on both ends, with a white belt around their middles, Dutch Belts stand out like flags in a clear sky.

"I like to have something that not everybody else has," says Farmer Daniels about his uncommon cows. There is another reason why he keeps them, though: the Dutch Belt is a rare breed, and Farmer Daniels wants to be sure it doesn't disappear. Dutch Belts have been a part of his life since he was a boy, when his father, who delivered milk to Hood, used to buy cows from the farmers on his rounds.

Dutch Belted cattle originated in Holland more than three hundred years ago. Their Dutch name is Lakenvelder, which means "sheeted," a reference to the fact that Dutch Belts look as though they've been wrapped with narrow white sheets. Dutch noblemen bred Lakenvelders for their distinctive markings because they wanted their cows to look different from common farmers'. Other belted animals became popular, too, including rabbits, chickens, goats, and pigs. By the end of the nineteenth century, however, Dutch Belted cows had fallen out of favor, and since the noblemen had prevented other farmers from having Dutch Belts, the future of the breed was in jeopardy. Today, in their Dutch homeland, only a few remain.

In the 1800s, the great showman P. T. Barnum imported some Dutch Belts to America to display in his circus. American dairy farmers soon discovered that these unusual-looking cows were quite good milkers. They can produce large quantities of milk, even as much as the popular Friesian, a modern dairy breed. The Dutch Belts' high-quality milk has tiny fat globules, almost as if it were already homogenized. It settles well on a baby's stomach, says Farmer Daniels, and its high butterfat content makes it ideal for use in other dairy products. Milk from his Dutch Belts goes to the Cabot Creamery in Vermont, where it is made into cheese and butter.

Inside the barn or out, Dutch Belted calves are frisky and full of spunk, but they grow up to be as even-tempered and gentle as their mothers. Their disposition makes them well suited for modern-day family farms. Paul Daniels remembers that not only his father but also his grandfather had Dutch Belted cows; the Vermont hills used to be dotted with rare breeds of cattle, he says. Perhaps one day they will be again.

Gloucester Old Spot Pig

A t Diamond Heart Farm, Nancy Daniels keeps a pair of pigs: Queen Anne and King George. They are Gloucester Old Spots, a rare breed from England. Gloucester Old Spots are large animals, with pinkish-white skin and a few black spots. Their huge lop ears hang over their eyes, making it hard for them to see where they're going; for this reason, Old Spots tend not to wander far. It's easy to keep them in their yards. When Queen Anne comes out of her barn for a walk, she wags her head from side to side, flapping her ears. Maybe this helps her to see better.

Gloucester Old Spots are good scavengers. They are sometimes called Orchard Pigs because they used to keep cider orchards clean by eating up the windfall apples. Farmers also traditionally fed whey, a by-product of the dairy industry, to their Gloucester Old Spots. Nancy feeds Queen Anne and King George milk from the Dutch Belted cows on the farm.

In the early 1900s, pig farmers liked Gloucester Old Spots because they were hardy and docile and produced high-quality meat without having to be fed expensive feed. Now, however, the number of Gloucester Old Spots has drastically declined. Pig farmers usually raise pigs for pork and bacon, but Nancy Daniels keeps hers for breeding. She is trying to increase the number of Gloucester Old Spots in this country, to save them from extinction. There are just a few breeders of these special pigs in America.

Female Gloucester Old Spots are good mothers to their offspring. They're calm and gentle, and unlike other sows, they allow people to get near their piglets. Queen Anne usually has a litter of piglets each spring and fall, and this year all of them have homes already. There are so few Old Spots available that people buy her piglets months before they're even born.

Guinea Hog

Guinea hogs are another rare and friendly breed of pig. Like Gloucester Old Spots, they're easy to care for and can live outdoors without much shelter. They grunt and chatter amiably with visitors. As with other pigs, stiff, broomlike bristles cover their thick skins.

Guinea hogs are only about half the size of Gloucester Old Spots. They grow to be fifteen to twenty inches tall and weigh just 150 to 300 pounds, which is not very big for a pig. Their compact bodies that are shaped like watermelons have dark-gray skin to protect them from sunburn, which is a problem for fair-skinned pigs such as Old Spots. Guinea hogs' prick ears stand up straight, probably enabling them to see better with their tiny eyes than Gloucester Old Spots.

Guinea hogs are supposed to have originated on the Guinea Coast of Africa; from there they were brought to America, France, Spain, and England through the slave trade. Because of their small size and gentle disposition, Guinea hogs make good backyard pigs. They used to be common on family farms in the southern United States, but now they're quite hard to find.

Deep in the Massachusetts woods, however, lives a busy Guinea hog foursome. Josephine, Henri, Napoleon, and Anastasi spend much of their time rooting around in the dirt with their snouts, digging up bugs, worms, and twigs to eat. Acting like natural bulldozers, they loosen the soil and pick out rocks and sticks. Farmers Margaret and Alan Marsh say that their Guinea hogs are helping them clear the woods and turn over the soil so they can plant a garden next spring.

Navajo-Churro Sheep

All kinds of sheep roam the pastures of southwestern America. If you look closely at a flock, you may see an unusual animal with four horns — two straightish and two curved. It will also have long, coarse, colored wool. This is the Churro sheep.

The word *churro* means "coarse wool" in Spanish. Spanish settlers brought these sheep with them from Spain to America in 1540. The animals provided the settlers with meat to eat and wool to weave into cloth. Churros were hardy enough to survive the harsh, snowy mountains and desert mesas of their new homeland. They needed little feed and could go for long periods without much water.

But after three hundred years in America, the Churro breed seemed doomed. By the mid-1800s, modern wool textile mills were making fine, machine-woven fabric that replaced coarse, hand-woven cloth. They used wool from white sheep — short, fine, and greasy — nothing like the Churro's, which was long, coarse, and nearly greaseless. People preferred the softer new fabrics, as well as the meat from the white lambs, which are generally fatter than the lean Churros. Newer breeds replaced the Churro, which very nearly became extinct.

But now, in the Chama Valley in New Mexico, ranchers like Antonio Manzanares are bringing back the old Churro breed. They're raising many kinds of sheep, including Churros and another rare breed called the Karakul. Seven-year-old Augustine Manzanares helps his father by herding their huge flock. Navajo Indians of the Southwest raise Churro sheep, too. The breed has become known as the Navajo-Churro or the Churro-Navajo. In the mid-1900s, the Indians lost most of their Churro sheep when the U.S. government had them slaughtered to prevent overgrazing. Today, both the Indians and the descendants of the Spanish settlers continue to weave Navajo-Churro wool into beautiful patterned rugs and blankets, and their designs have been famous the world over for centuries. Weavers like Churro wool because it spins easily, absorbs dyes well, and makes sturdy cloth.

Sheep and wool are still a way of life in the tiny town of Los Ojos, where Augustine lives. His mother helps run a community wool shop, called Tierra Wools. Local weavers are reviving the family traditions of hand-spinning, dyeing, and weaving. They make and sell colorful rugs, jackets, and pillows from their beloved Churros' wool.

The six big floor-looms in the shop creak and thump as the weavers throw their shuttles back and forth. Sometimes they work from designs that their ancestors used; sometimes they create new ones of their own. The youngest weaver is twelve-year-old Ana. She sells her woven mats almost as fast as she can make them. Today, customers from distant cities once again buy products made from Churro wool, just as they did over a hundred years ago.

American Mammoth Jackstock

L ong, long ears like a jackrabbit's frame the gentle face of the American Mammoth jackstock. From the tip of one ear to the tip of the other is a span of over thirty-three inches, giving jackstock an appropriate nickname that they share with donkeys — "Longears."

Like donkeys, jackstock also have short, upright manes, tufted tails like a lion's, and a braying voice. But even though jackstock and donkeys look and sound very much alike, they are actually two different breeds of the same animal, the ass.

The American Mammoth jackstock is the largest breed of ass in the world. Standing at least fifty-six inches high at the shoulder, jackstock can weigh over a thousand pounds, more than the weight of five grown men.

Two jackstock live at Random Hills Farm in New Hampshire. Lucy is a gray Mammoth jenny, a female ass. Treasure, her foal, is a black Mammoth jack, a male ass. When he was first born, Treasure could walk under Lucy's belly. Now, at one year old, he's nearly as tall as she is.

Lucy came to the farm completely untrained, but not long after her arrival, ten-year-old Rebecca Tolman and her younger sister Emily were riding her on trails in the woods. Rebecca's parents chose a Mammoth for them to ride instead of a horse because horses can be difficult for beginners to handle. Mammoth jackstock make calm, safe, intelligent mounts. What could be mistaken for stubbornness is more likely a sign of how smart Mammoth jackstock really are. "They will stop and look and think," says Rebecca's mother. No matter how much you urge her, Lucy won't slog through a stretch of boggy pasture. She knows better. In that way, jackstock are trustworthy. They don't get themselves or their riders into trouble.

The American Mammoth jackstock was originally used for breeding mules. A mule is the offspring of a female horse, called a mare, and a jack. Because of their size, Mammoth jacks produce large pack and draft mules when they are bred to draft-horse mares. The famous "twenty-mule team" mules that hauled wagonloads of the mineral borax from mines in the American West were quite likely bred from Mammoth jacks.

The Mammoth jackstock is the only ass that is truly an American breed. Its ancestors were Spanish asses, especially the Catalonian. Late in the 1700s, General George Washington received a fine jack as a gift from the king of Spain. At the time, there was a law in Spain forbidding the export of asses. Whether or not this particular jack was an ancestor of the American Mammoth breed is uncertain, but the first President of the United States obviously knew the value of a good jack for producing mules: Washington earned $678 by breeding him to mares throughout the South.

Although Mammoth jackstock are fairly common in some parts of the country, such as Tennessee, Missouri, Kentucky, and Texas, they are rare in the Northeast. Before getting Lucy, the Tolmans had never even seen a Mammoth jackstock, and there are no Mammoth jacks in the New England area for them to breed Lucy to. Now that mules have been replaced by tractors in America, there has been a serious decline in jackstock, and there are fewer than two hundred purebred Mammoth jacks listed in the breed's registry. In the future, however, as we search for alternatives to expensive, polluting fuel-powered farm machinery, Mammoth jackstock and their large mule offspring may provide a fitting answer.

Ancona and Black Australorp Chickens

Every evening, around suppertime, eight-year-old Lindsay Craig scoops a handful of scratch from the feed sack in his backyard henhouse and scatters it about for the chickens. A colorful flock of hens peck at the treat of cracked corn and sunflower seeds while Lindsay collects their eggs. He brings a basketful to his mother, Suze. She cooks with them or sells them to the neighbors, fresh every day.

These are not ordinary eggs. They look as though they've been painted for Easter in pastel shades of pinky white, pale green, and honey brown. The eggs are from a mixed flock of poultry; each breed lays a different color. Although some of the hens in the Craigs' flock are common in America, two of their breeds — the Black Australorp and the Ancona — are not.

"As long as we have hens, we want hens that are interesting to look at," says Suze. "And they are the most marvelous garbage disposal. Nothing is wasted." The hens eat all the family's leftovers, except for citrus fruit, tea leaves, and coffee grounds. Every Halloween they get the extra pumpkins from the pumpkin patch.

In the early 1900s, Black Australorps could be found on many American farms. They originally came from Australia, where a Black Australorp hen once achieved a world record by laying 364 eggs in 365 days. Black Australorps are fairly calm birds; Lindsay can persuade one to let him hold her and stroke her beetle-green and black feathers.

Not all of the chickens are so tame. Anconas are skittish. These snappy-looking black-and-white birds avoid capture with clever quickness; raccoons, foxes, and even the butcher can't catch an Ancona that doesn't want to be caught. Anconas are an Italian breed that used to be popular in Europe for egg laying. They were brought to America in the 1800s.

Each spring, Lindsay and his mother order a new flock of assorted chickens from a hatchery, a farm where chicken eggs are hatched. A noisy boxful of day-old chicks arrives at the post office in mid-April. Hatcheries can help keep old-fashioned poultry breeds from going extinct, but only if families such as the Craigs are willing and able to raise them.

American Bashkir Curly Horse

No one knows exactly where horses with curly coats first came from. Some people believe that either the Mongols or the Russians brought them to the western coast of North America over the Bering Strait. Others say that the curly horses came from Spain; if that's true, then these mysterious animals could be related to the wild Spanish mustang ponies of the American West. In fact, some curlies still roam the plains of Nevada, Oregon, and Wyoming along with mustangs, and in the 1800s, American Plains Indians drew pictures of the curly horses they rode.

Curly horses are named after Bashkir, a region of the Ural Mountains, in Russia. However, it is unclear whether they are really related to the Russian breed of horse called the Bashkir, which is used for transportation, drafting power, milk, and meat. Some people think American curly-coated horses are more likely related to a Russian breed called the Lokai, which also has a curly coat. But whatever their ancestry, curly-haired horses have probably been around for centuries.

Their unusual locks make some people think of enchanting mythical beasts, but others find curly horses just plain ugly. P. T. Barnum called the curly a "freak of nature" and he exhibited one in his circus as an animal oddity, just as he did with the Dutch Belted cow. Some ranchers disliked the curlies' looks so much that they slaughtered them; as a result, their numbers dwindled.

But there are people who love these rare horses, and who are slowly bringing them back as a respected breed. Peter Damele, a Nevada horseman, established the first large herd of American Bashkir Curlies early in the 1900s. Today, Bashkir Curly owners keep careful track of their horses by listing the animals' names in a national registry. Some prefer to call them simply American Curly horses.

About twenty curly-coated horses of all different colors live at Top o' the Hill Farm in Vermont. There are creamy-gold palominos, spotted pintos, and reddish-brown chestnuts. Their coats vary in curliness from kinky waves to tight ringlets.

Eleven-year-old Zoe helps to care for the curlies that her mother breeds at Top o' the Hill Farm, making sure they have plenty of water to drink. Curly horses are easy to keep. Their long coats and extra layers of body fat enable them to live outdoors year-round, even during the freezing Vermont winters. Unlike most domestic horse breeds, curlies don't require grain; they're satisfied with a simple diet of grass and hay. Nor do they need shoes for their sturdy, round hooves.

Curlies shed their crinkly coats in the summer and look like straight-haired horses until their curls grow back again the next winter. In February, Dream Curl was a ringlet-covered white mare, but by May her curls were gone and she was a sleek, golden palomino with a crinkly-coated foal named Dream Come True. Most of the curls form on the horses' neck, on their back, in their ears, and sometimes around their fetlocks.

American Curlies are known for being strong, intelligent, and alert, even though the shape of their eyes sometimes makes them look sleepy. They're also unusually calm and easily trained.

"They're an all-purpose horse," says Zoe's mother. She has seen curlies perform well in tough rodeo events as well as in fancy sidesaddle and jumping classes at horse shows. It seems that the curly's coat no longer makes him an outcast. Instead, it's a sign that there is a friendly, versatile horse underneath.

A fter conducting a census of North American livestock breeds in 1985, the American Minor Breeds Conservancy (AMBC) compiled the following list of farm animals that are in danger of extinction. For an updated list, write to the American Minor Breeds Conservancy, P.O. Box 477, Pittsboro, NC 27312.

CATTLE

Ayrshire cattle
Beef Devon cattle
Belted Galloway cattle
Canadienne cattle
Dexter cattle
Dutch Belted cattle
Florida/Pineywoods cattle
Guernsey cattle
Kerry cattle
Lineback cattle
Milking Devon cattle
Milking Shorthorn cattle
Red Poll cattle
Scotch Highland cattle
White Park cattle

Scotch Highland cow

GOATS

Fainting goats
Nigerian Dwarf goats
San Clemente goats

Devon calf

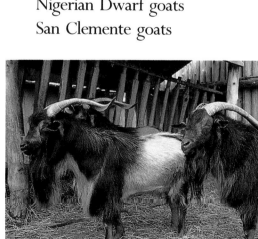

San Clemente goats

ASSES

- American Mammoth jackstock
- Burros
- Donkeys
- Poitou asses
- Spotted asses

Tamworth pigs

PIGS

- Berkshire pigs
- Gloucester Old Spot pigs
- Guinea hogs
- Large Black pigs
- Mulefoot hogs
- Ossabaw Island hogs
- Poland China pigs
- Tamworth pigs

SHEEP

- Barbados sheep
- Border Leicester sheep
- Cheviot sheep
- Cotswold sheep
- Delaine Merino sheep
- Dorset Horn sheep
- Gulf Coast Native sheep
- Hog Island sheep
- Jacob sheep
- Karakul sheep
- Leicester Longwool sheep
- Lincoln Longwool sheep
- Navajo-Churro sheep
- Oxford sheep
- Santa Cruz sheep
- Shetland sheep
- Shropshire sheep
- Southdown sheep
- Tunis sheep
- Wiltshire Horn sheep

Jacob sheep

Percheron horses

HORSES

American Bashkir Curly
horses
American Cream Draft
horses
Belgian horses
Canadian horses
Cleveland Bay horses
Clydesdale horses
Exmoor ponies
Gotland horses
Hackney horses
Lipizzan horses
Percheron horses
Przewalski horses
Shire horses
Spanish mustangs
Suffolk Punch horses
Tarpan horses
Wild mustangs

POULTRY

Ancona chickens
Barred Plymouth Rock
chickens
Black Australorp chickens
Black Jersey Giant chickens
Black Minorca chickens
Brown Leghorn chickens
Delaware chickens
*Dorking chickens
Khaki Campbell ducks
New Hampshire chickens
Pilgrim geese
Rhode Island Red chickens
Rouen ducks
Toulouse geese
White Jersey Giant chickens
White Wyandotte chickens

White Jersey Giant chicken
(rooster)

*Dorking chickens are not on the AMBC list, but they are included here as an example of one of many poultry breeds considered endangered by the Society for the Preservation of Poultry Antiquities.

Dorking chicken (hen)